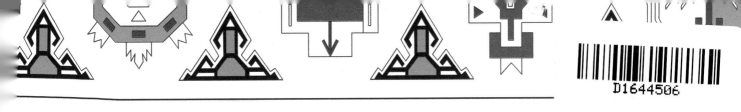

Flags of the World

to colour

Written by Susan Meredith

Designed and illustrated by Ian McNee and Hope Reynolds

Maps by Craig Asquith and Anna Gould

Flags consultant: Jos Poels

Contents

About flags

This book shows the national flag of every independent country in the world. The flags are grouped by the six continents, which you can see on this map.

Designs

Flags are designed to be eye-catching, usually with bold colours and simple patterns, so they don't look too distorted when they're flying in the wind.

Many flags simply have three bright stripes. They are known as 'tricolours' and were inspired by the French flag.

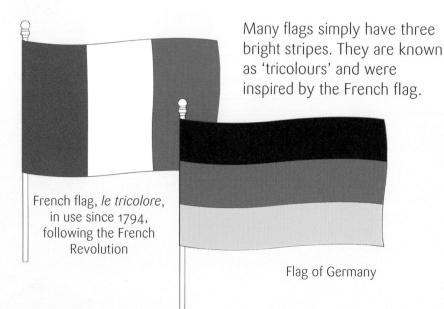

French flag, *le tricolore*, in use since 1794, following the French Revolution

Flag of Germany

NORTH AMERICA

Atlantic Ocean

SOUTH AMERICA

Emblems

Some flags include the country's national emblem or coat of arms.

The emblem on the Argentinian flag is the 'Sun of May', which commemorates a revolution in May 1810.

Colours

Often, nobody knows why a flag was given its particular design or colours, especially if it's been in use for a long time. But some colours are associated with these meanings:

Sea
Sky
Rivers

Purity
Peace
Snow

Courage
Vitality
Revolution
Communism

Life
Nature
Fertile land
Islam

Determination
Strength

Wealth
Sunshine

EUROPE

ASIA

AFRICA

Pacific Ocean

Indian Ocean

OCEANIA

Similar flags

Some countries have similar flags because they have had political or economic links in the past.

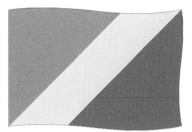

Flag of Congo

Several African flags are red, green and yellow. These colours have become known as Pan-African, meaning 'all over Africa'.

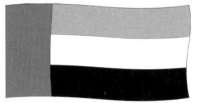

Flag of United Arab Emirates

The flags of Arab countries, mainly in North Africa and Western Asia, are often red, green, black and white. These are known as Pan-Arab colours.

Competitions

If a government decides to change its country's flag, a design competition may be held.

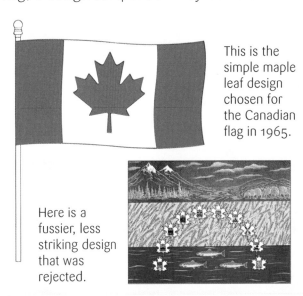

This is the simple maple leaf design chosen for the Canadian flag in 1965.

Here is a fussier, less striking design that was rejected.

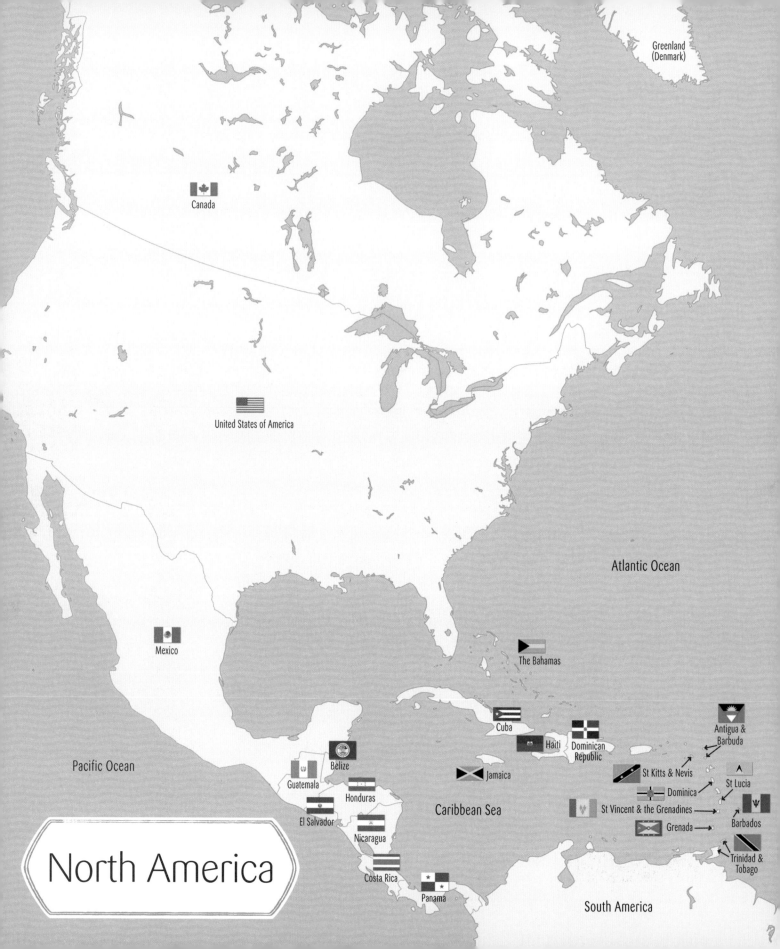

Greenland
(Denmark)

Canada

United States of America

Atlantic Ocean

Mexico

The Bahamas

Pacific Ocean

Cuba

Haiti

Dominican
Republic

Antigua &
Barbuda

Belize

Guatemala

Jamaica

St Kitts & Nevis

St Lucia

Honduras

Dominica

El Salvador

Caribbean Sea

St Vincent & the Grenadines

Nicaragua

Barbados

Grenada

Costa Rica

Trinidad &
Tobago

Panama

South America

North America

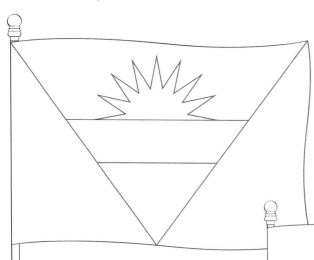

Antigua and Barbuda

On this flag, black stands for the African ancestry of the people, red for energy, blue for sea, and white for sand. The sun represents the dawn of a new era, when the country became independent of Britain in 1967.

Antigua and Barbuda

Canada

Canada is famous for its maple trees. The maple leaf is its national emblem.

Canada

Barbados

Belize

The coat of arms on Belize's flag shows symbols of the country's history in the timber trade. The motto means, 'I flourish in the shade' in Latin.

Belize

The Bahamas

The blue and yellow on the flag of the Bahamas represent sea and sand, while the black triangle symbolizes determination.

The Bahamas

Dominica

Dominica

This flag features Dominica's national bird, the sisserou parrot. The stars represent the country's ten regions.

Cuba

Cuba

Cuba's flag is nicknamed the 'Lone Star', in contrast with the US flag, which has 50 stars.

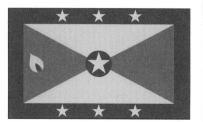

Grenada

Grenada

The flame shape is actually a nutmeg, the main crop of Grenada. The central star represents the capital city – St George's – and the outer stars, the country's six regions.

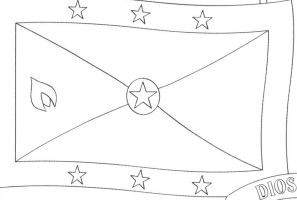

Dominican Republic

Dominican Republic

The book in the emblem is a Bible, which is said to be open at a page which reads, 'And the truth shall set you free'.

Haiti

The coat of arms depicts the Haitian victory over French rule in 1803. The cap above the palm tree symbolizes liberty, while the French motto means, 'Unity is strength'.

L'UNION FAIT LA FORCE

Haiti

Costa Rica

Honduras

Guatemala

Jamaica

Costa Rica

The red, white and blue stripes of this flag were inspired by the French *tricolore* and the ideals of the French Revolution – liberty, equality, fraternity.

Jamaica

A saying explains the meaning of this flag: 'There may be burdens and hardships (black) but we have hope (green) and the sun still shines (yellow).' In some versions, 'we have hope' is replaced with 'the land is green'.

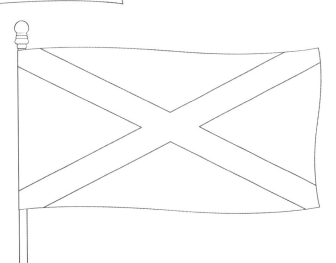

7

Mexico

Mexico

The emblem on the Mexican flag shows an eagle balancing on a cactus plant on an island in a lake, while eating a snake. This is from a story about the founding of Mexico City.

Nicaragua

Saint Kitts and Nevis

Saint Kitts and Nevis

The two stars on the central stripe stand for hope and freedom.

El Salvador

El Salvador

The date on the emblem refers to the day El Salvador became independent from Spain. The red cap stands for liberty, as on the Haitian flag. The rainbow symbolizes peace, and the laurel wreath, unity.

United States of America

Known as the 'Stars and Stripes', the US flag has 13 stripes, representing the original 13 states, and 50 stars, representing the current 50 states.

Saint Lucia

The Saint Lucian flag symbolizes the island's volcanic mountains, beaches and seas. The black and white stand for different races living in peace.

United States of America

Panama

Trinidad and Tobago

Saint Lucia

Saint Vincent and the Grenadines

Saint Vincent and the Grenadines

The diamonds refer to the islands' nickname, the 'Gems of the Antilles' – a bigger group of islands of which they are said to be the most beautiful. The V-shape stands for Vincent.

Venezuela

Guyana

Suriname

French Guiana
(France)

Colombia

Ecuador

Peru

Brazil

Bolivia

Paraguay

Chile

Pacific Ocean

Argentina

Uruguay

Atlantic Ocean

South America

Bolivia

Red stands for bravery, yellow for Bolivia's mineral wealth, and green for the fertility of the land.

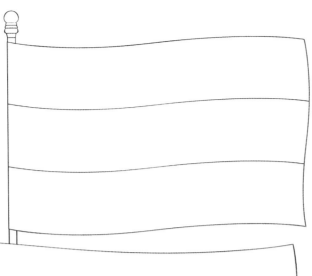

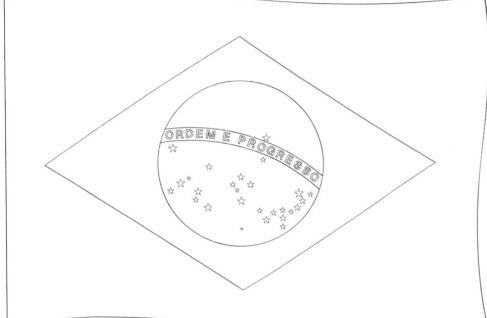

Brazil

The emblem represents the night sky over Brazil, while the motto says 'Order and progress' in Portuguese, the language spoken in the country.

Colombia

A children's song about the flag goes: 'Yellow is our gold, blue our vast seas, and red the blood that gave us our freedom.' Colombia became independent of Spain in 1810.

Bolivia

Venezuela

Brazil

Chile

Colombia

Ecuador

Ecuador

This coat of arms shows the River Guayas, flowing from Mount Chimborazo, the highest mountain in Ecuador. An Andean condor, a large vulture that lives in the Andes Mountains, is perched above.

Peru

Paraguay

Paraguay

This is the only national flag with a different emblem on each side.

Paraguay

Front

The star stands for Paraguay's revolution against Spanish rule and the declaration of independence that was made in 1811.

Back

The lion is guarding the red cap which symbolizes liberty. The motto says 'Peace and justice' in Spanish.

Suriname

This flag was first used in 1975, when Suriname became independent of the Netherlands. The star symbolizes unity.

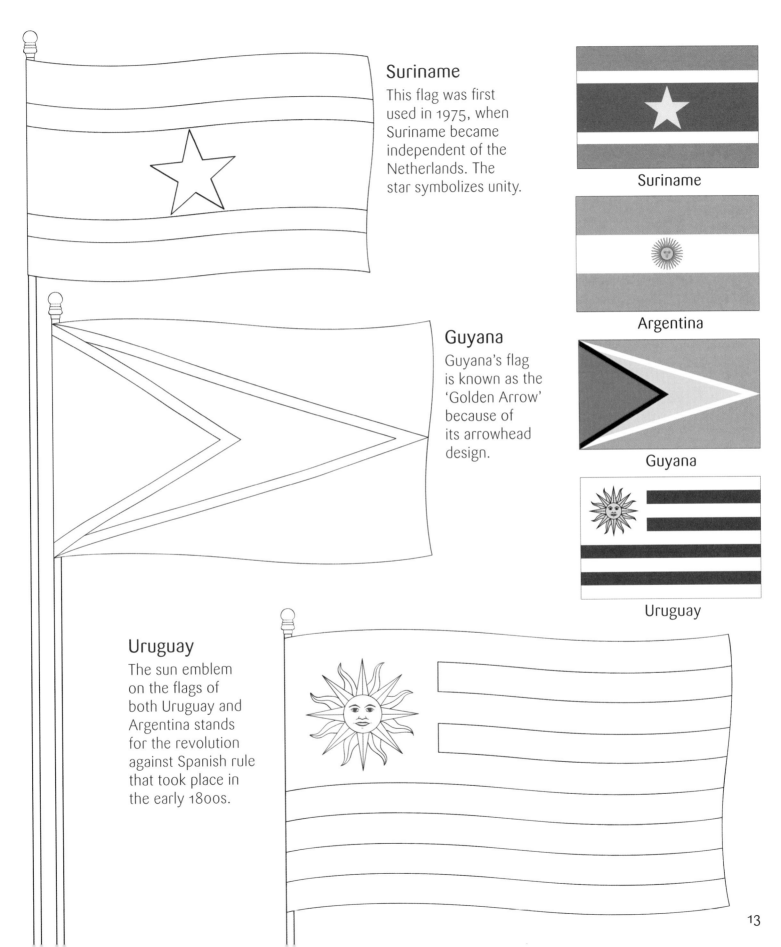

Suriname

Argentina

Guyana

Uruguay

Guyana

Guyana's flag is known as the 'Golden Arrow' because of its arrowhead design.

Uruguay

The sun emblem on the flags of both Uruguay and Argentina stands for the revolution against Spanish rule that took place in the early 1800s.

Europe

Arctic Ocean

Iceland

Sweden

Finland

Norway

Russia

Estonia

Latvia

Denmark

Lithuania

Russia

Belarus

Ireland

United Kingdom

Netherlands

Poland

Belgium

Germany

Ukraine

Atlantic Ocean

Luxembourg

Czechia

Slovakia

France

Slovenia

Austria

Moldova

Switzerland

Liechtenstein

Hungary

Romania

Slovenia

Croatia

Monaco

San Marino

Bosnia & Herzegovina

Serbia

Black Sea

Portugal

Andorra

Vatican City

Montenegro

Kosovo

Bulgaria

Turkey

Spain

Macedonia

Asia

Italy

Albania

Greece

← Malta

Cyprus

Mediterranean Sea

Africa

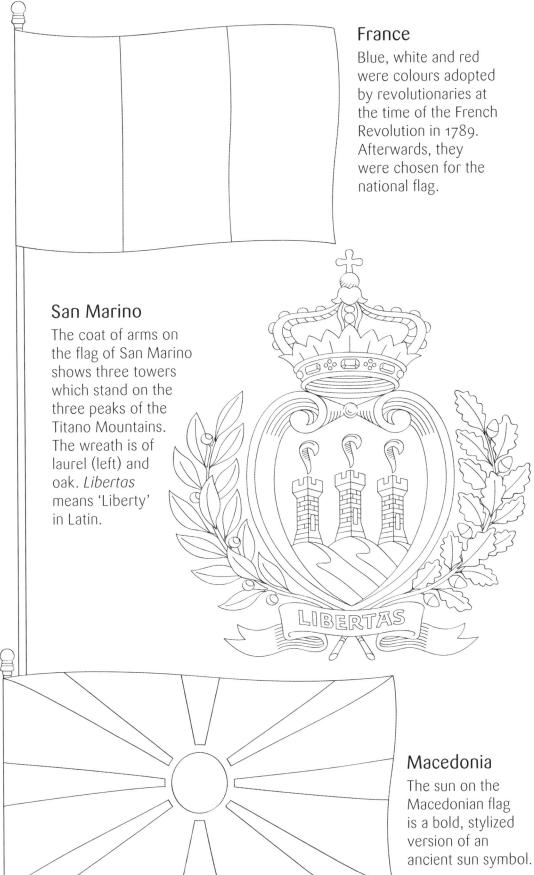

France

Blue, white and red were colours adopted by revolutionaries at the time of the French Revolution in 1789. Afterwards, they were chosen for the national flag.

France

San Marino

The coat of arms on the flag of San Marino shows three towers which stand on the three peaks of the Titano Mountains. The wreath is of laurel (left) and oak. *Libertas* means 'Liberty' in Latin.

San Marino

Latvia

Kosovo

Macedonia

The sun on the Macedonian flag is a bold, stylized version of an ancient sun symbol.

Macedonia

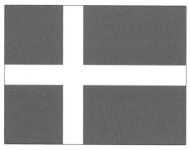

Denmark

Ireland

Russia

Andorra

Lithuania

Denmark

The Danish flag is one of the oldest national flags. Nearby countries in northern Europe – Norway, Sweden, Finland and Iceland – copied the cross design for their own flags.

Andorra

The coat of arms on Andorra's flag includes a bishop's mitre (hat), two cows and a Latin motto: 'United virtue is stronger.'

Lithuania

The flag design was based on the colours of Lithuania's traditional costume.

16

Spain

The words *Plus ultra* on the coat of arms mean 'Further beyond' in Latin. This was the motto of King Charles V of Spain who built a huge empire in the 16th century.

Spain

Bulgaria

Greece

United Kingdom

Poland

United Kingdom

The 'Union flag' is the flag of the United Kingdom of England, Scotland, Wales and Northern Ireland.

Poland

Polish children learn a rhyme which includes the lines: 'And on this flag there's white and red. Red for love, white for a pure heart.' The flag is like Monaco's and Indonesia's but the other way up.

Cyprus

Ukraine

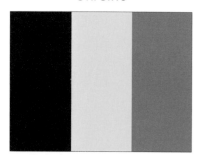

Belgium

Turkey

Croatia

Cyprus

The flag of Cyprus shows an outline map of the island. The two olive branches and the white background symbolize peace.

Ukraine

The blue and yellow stripes on this flag are said to stand for blue sky over golden wheatfields.

Croatia

Historically, Croatia was made up of five regions, so there are five shields at the top of the coat of arms. The check pattern was a symbol of Croatian kings in the Middle Ages.

Moldova

Moldova used to be part of Romania. Its flag has the same stripes as Romania's but includes the Moldovan coat of arms, showing an eagle and a wild ox's head.

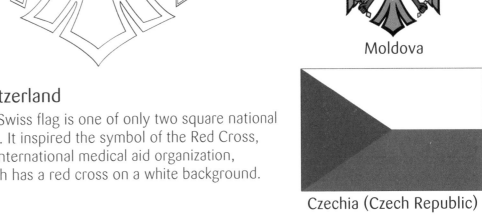

Switzerland

The Swiss flag is one of only two square national flags. It inspired the symbol of the Red Cross, the international medical aid organization, which has a red cross on a white background.

Bosnia and Herzegovina

The triangle on this flag represents the three native peoples of the country - Bosniaks, Serbs and Croats. Its yellow colour symbolizes hope, and the blue background and stars stand for Europe.

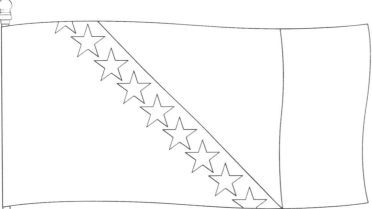

Hungary

Moldova

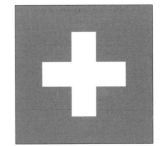
Czechia (Czech Republic)

Switzerland

Bosnia and Herzegovina

19

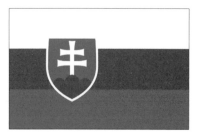

Slovakia

Montenegro

Luxembourg

Italy

Norway

Slovenia

Montenegro

The coat of arms on Montenegro's flag includes a double-headed eagle and a lion. It's based on a banner used by the country's only king, Nikolai I, who ruled from 1910 to 1918.

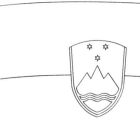

Norway

Norway's flag is very similar to Iceland's but with the colours swapped around.

Slovenia

Slovenia's coat of arms shows the highest mountain range in the country, the three-peaked Triglav.

Albania

The Albanian flag is based on the flag of Skanderbeg, a national hero in the 15th century. In one of the local languages, Albania means 'Land of the Eagles'.

Albania

Austria

Malta

The symbol in the corner shows the George Cross, a British award given to the people of Malta for their bravery during the Second World War.

Malta

Sweden

Portugal

Portugal was one of the first countries whose sailors explored the world. The yellow sphere behind the coat of arms is an early type of ship's navigating instrument.

Portugal

Germany

Vatican City

Estonia

Monaco

Iceland

Germany

Germany's flag has the same colours as Belgium's, but in a different order and running horizontally instead of vertically.

Vatican City

Vatican City State is the headquarters of the Roman Catholic Church. The keys on its flag symbolize the keys to the kingdom of heaven.

Iceland

Red stands for Iceland's fiery volcanoes, white for its snow, and blue for its mountains.

Serbia

Serbia's coat of arms includes a double-headed eagle, an ancient symbol often used to indicate strength and power. The crown refers to the time when Serbia was ruled by kings.

Netherlands

The top stripe of the Netherlands' flag was originally orange. In the 1600s it was changed to red, but no one now knows why.

Belarus

Serbia

Romania

Finland

Netherlands

Liechtenstein

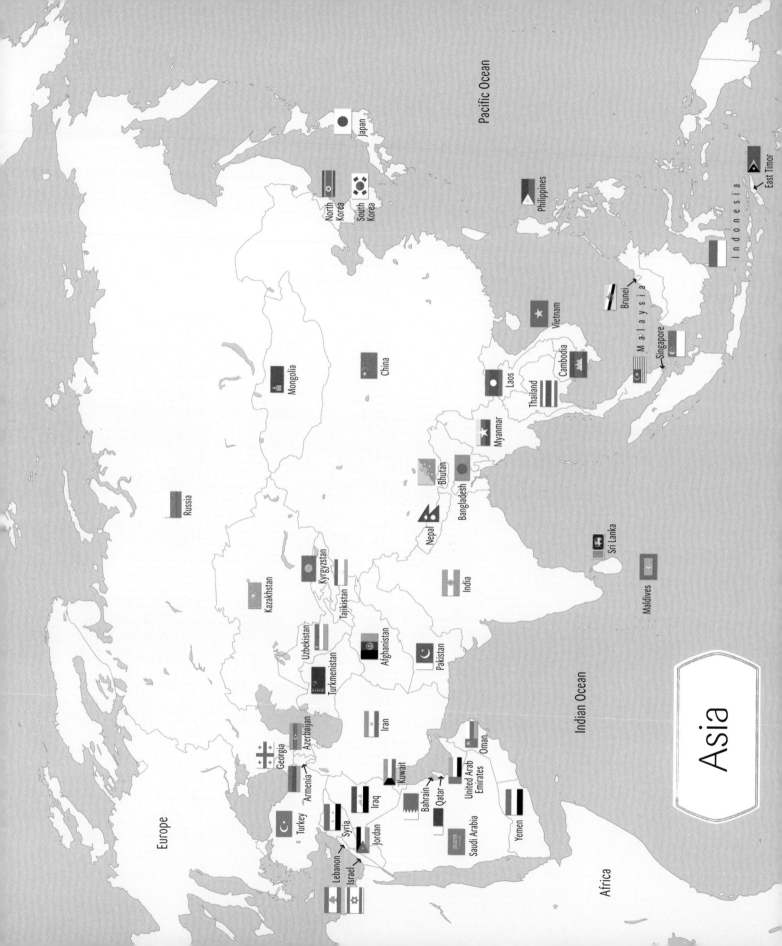

Asia

Pacific Ocean

Indian Ocean

Europe

Africa

Japan

North Korea

South Korea

Philippines

East Timor

Indonesia

Brunei

Malaysia

Vietnam

Singapore

China

Mongolia

Cambodia

Laos

Thailand

Myanmar

Bhutan

Bangladesh

Russia

Nepal

Sri Lanka

Kyrgyzstan

India

Kazakhstan

Tajikistan

Maldives

Uzbekistan

Turkmenistan

Afghanistan

Pakistan

Iran

Azerbaijan

Georgia

Oman

Armenia

Kuwait

United Arab Emirates

Turkey

Iraq

Bahrain

Qatar

Syria

Jordan

Saudi Arabia

Yemen

Lebanon

Israel

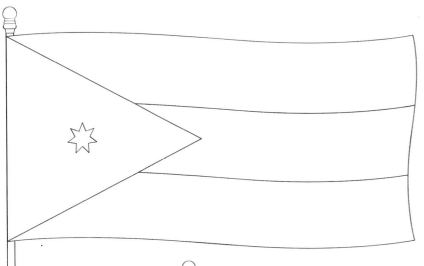

Jordan

The seven-pointed star on Jordan's flag represents the opening seven verses of the Qur'an, the Muslim holy book.

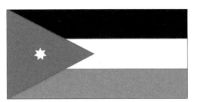

Jordan

Iran

Malaysia

The star and crescent are Muslim symbols, showing that Malaysia is a Muslim country. The flag is similar to the US flag, in that the 14 stripes represent the 14 states of Malaysia.

Malaysia

Qatar

Bhutan

In Bhutan, thunder is said to be the voices of dragons roaring. Bhutan means 'Land of the Thunder Dragon'.

Bhutan

Saudi Arabia

Kazakhstan

North Korea

Afghanistan

Tajikistan

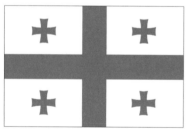

Georgia

Russia

Kazakhstan

The motif down the side of the flag is a traditional Kazakh pattern, seen on everything from furniture to jewellery. The eagle stands for freedom.

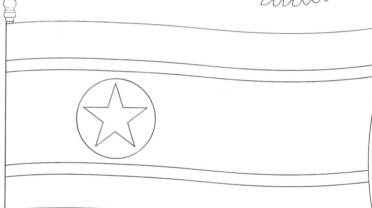

North Korea

The colours of the flag are traditional in Korean culture and the red star stands for the country's communism.

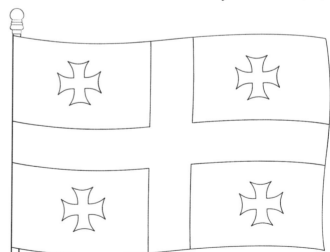

Georgia

Georgia's flag has its origins back in the Middle Ages. The large red cross is the flag of Saint George, the country's patron saint.

Israel

The emblem on Israel's flag is known as the 'Star of David', an important Jewish symbol.

Israel

Indonesia

Pakistan

The star and crescent indicate that Pakistan is a Muslim country. The green background stands for the Muslim people, the white stripe for the smaller number of people who follow other religions.

Pakistan

Iraq

Lebanon

Lebanon

The cedar tree has been associated with Lebanon for thousands of years. The country used to be covered in huge cedar forests.

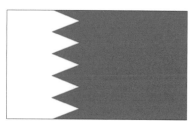

Bahrain

Azerbaijan

Oman

Vietnam

United Arab Emirates

Cambodia

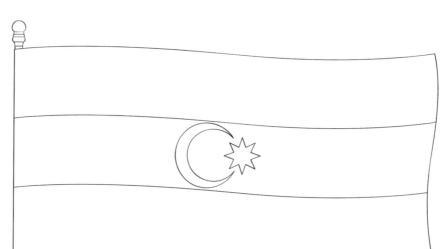

Azerbaijan

Blue stands for the people of Western Asia, red for progress, green and the crescent and star for Islam.

Vietnam

The five points of the star on Vietnam's flag represent the country's workers, farmers, intellectuals, soldiers and young people.

Cambodia

Cambodia's flag is the only one to show a famous building – the huge temple of Angkor Wat.

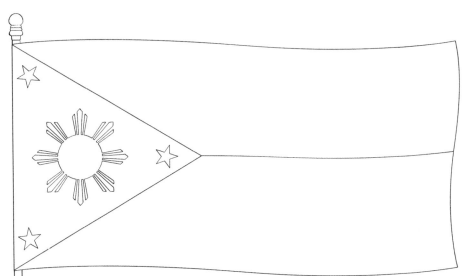

Philippines

The Philippines is the only country to fly its flag upside down when it is at war. Other countries have separate war flags.

Nepal

This is the only national flag that is an irregular shape. The symbols represent the hope that Nepal will last as long as the sun and moon are in the sky.

Mongolia

The symbol on the flag is called the Soyombo. It is seen all over Mongolia.

Philippines

Brunei

Bangladesh

Syria

Nepal

Mongolia

Myanmar (Burma)

China

Turkmenistan

Singapore

Kuwait

Japan

Turkmenistan

Turkmenistan is famous for its carpets. The patterns down the side of the flag are carpet designs, known as 'guls'.

Myanmar (Burma)

The yellow stands for team spirit, green for peace, and red for courage.

Kuwait

Kuwait's is the only national flag to have a cut-off triangle at the side.

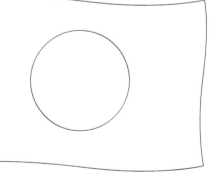

Japan

Japan means 'Land of the Rising Sun', which is why the flag shows a red circle.

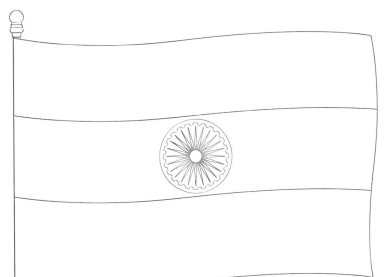

India

The wheel in the middle of India's flag is called the Ashoka Chakra. It is an ancient Indian symbol of life and continuity.

India

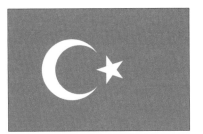

Turkey

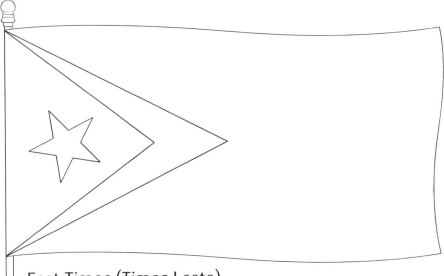

East Timor (Timor-Leste)

The red background symbolizes East Timor's struggle for independence, first from Portugal, then from Indonesia.

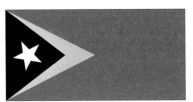

East Timor (Timor-Leste)

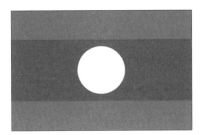

Laos

Kyrgyzstan

The pattern in the middle of the flag shows the roof of a yurt – a type of tent, the traditional home of the Kyrgyz people.

Uzbekistan

Kyrgyzstan

Maldives

Sri Lanka

Yemen

Armenia

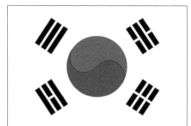

South Korea

Thailand

Sri Lanka

Sri Lanka has a mixed population – the dark red background and leaves stand for its Buddhists, the green stripe for Muslims, and the orange for Tamils. The lion symbolizes bravery.

Armenia

Red symbolizes the independence of the people, orange their talent and hard work, and blue their wish to live peacefully under blue skies.

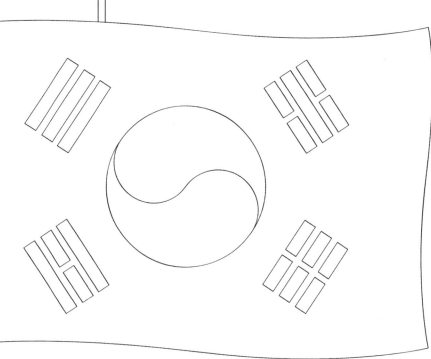

South Korea

The circle on the South Korean flag is the Yin-Yang symbol, representing the harmony of opposites in Eastern philosophy. The four black symbols stand for heaven, earth, fire and water.

Morocco

Tunisia

Mediterranean Sea

Asia

Algeria

Libya

Egypt

Western Sahara
(Morocco)

Mauritania

Mali

Niger

Sudan

Eritrea

Cape Verde

Chad

Djibouti

Senegal

The Gambia

Guinea-Bissau

Guinea

Burkina Faso

Benin

Nigeria

Central African Republic

South Sudan

Ethiopia

Somalia

Sierra Leone

Liberia

Ivory Coast

Ghana

Togo

Cameroon

Equatorial Guinea

São Tomé & Príncipe

Gabon

Congo

Congo
(Democratic Republic)

Rwanda

Burundi

Uganda

Kenya

Indian Ocean

Seychelles

Tanzania

Angola

Zambia

Malawi

Mozambique

Comoros

Madagascar

Mauritius

Atlantic Ocean

Zimbabwe

Namibia

Botswana

Swaziland

South
Africa

Lesotho

Africa

Ethiopia

Mauritania

Chad

Sudan

Gabon

Angola

Ethiopia

Ethiopia was the first African country to choose red, green and yellow for its flag. So many others copied the colours, they became known as Pan-African (all Africa) colours.

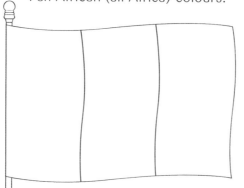

Chad

Chad's flag is almost identical to Romania's. The blue stripe on Chad's is a slightly darker shade, but it's hard to spot the difference.

Gabon

Green stands for the huge forests and national parks of Gabon, yellow for its hot, sunny climate, and blue for its coastline.

Angola

The segment of wheel on Angola's flag stands for factory workers, the knife for farm workers, and the star for solidarity and progress.

South Africa

The green Y-shape symbolizes people who were once separate coming together and following the same path into the future.

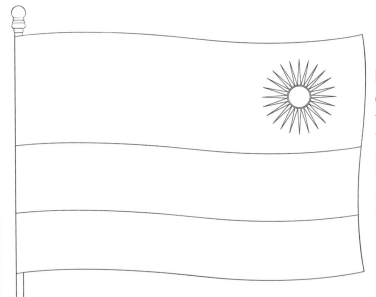

Liberia

The design is similar to the US 'Stars and Stripes'. Many settlers in Liberia were freed African-American slaves.

Rwanda

On the Rwandan flag, blue stands for happiness and peace, yellow for economic development, and green for prosperity. The sun symbolizes enlightenment.

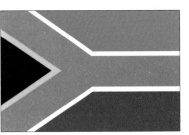

South Africa

Ghana

Nigeria

Liberia

Burkina Faso

Rwanda

35

Burundi

Djibouti

Botswana

Senegal

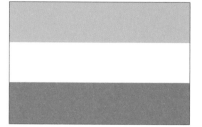

Sierra Leone

Seychelles

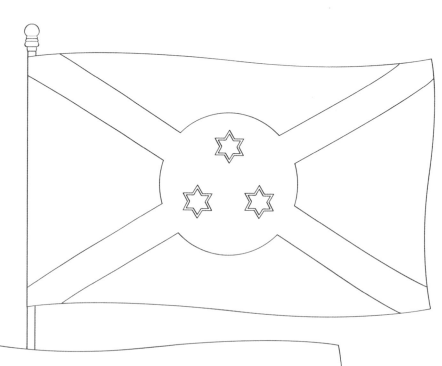

Burundi

The three stars on the flag of Burundi stand for 'Unity, work, progress' – the national motto.

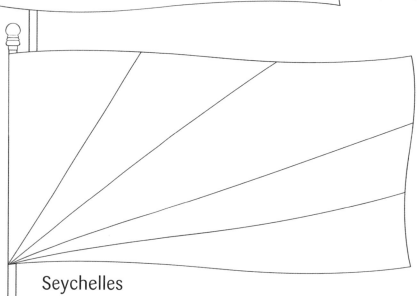

Botswana

The blue represents much-needed rain. The black and white stripes are inspired by zebras, the country's national animal, and stand for harmony between black and white people.

Seychelles

The unusual design of the Seychelles' flag is intended to convey dynamism and hope for the future.

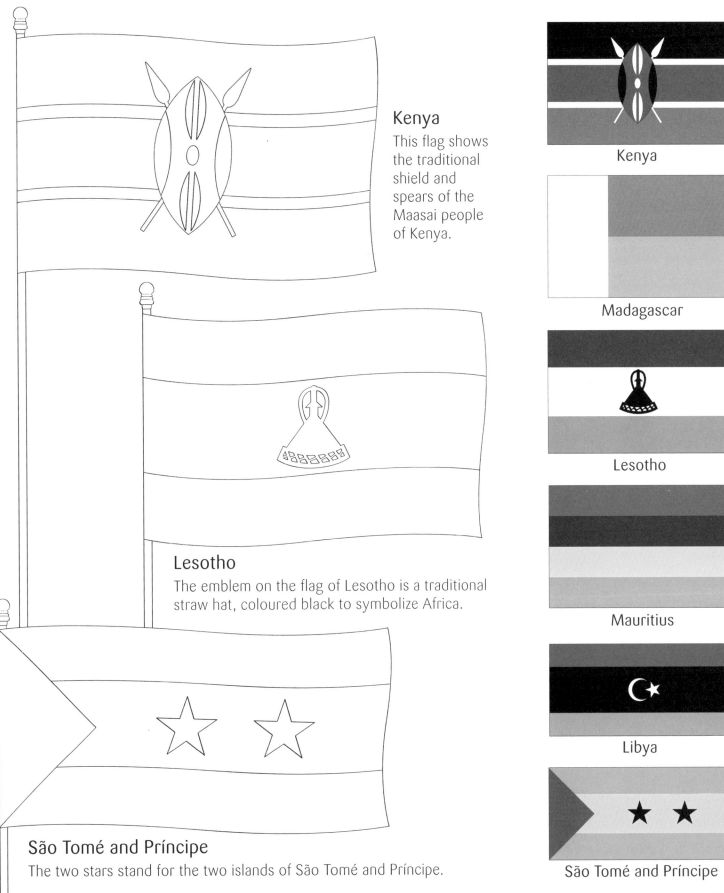

Kenya

This flag shows the traditional shield and spears of the Maasai people of Kenya.

Kenya

Madagascar

Lesotho

The emblem on the flag of Lesotho is a traditional straw hat, coloured black to symbolize Africa.

Lesotho

Mauritius

Libya

São Tomé and Príncipe

The two stars stand for the two islands of São Tomé and Príncipe.

São Tomé and Príncipe

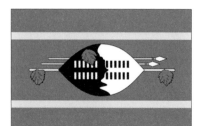

Swaziland

Congo

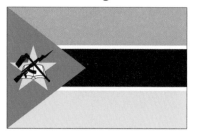

Mozambique

Somalia

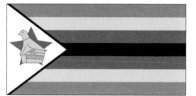

Zimbabwe

Ivory Coast (Côte d'Ivoire)

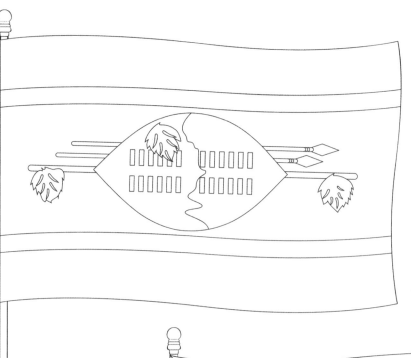

Swaziland

The Swazi flag shows a shield, two traditional warriors' spears and a fighting stick, with tassels. The shield is black and white to symbolize black and white people living together in peace.

Mozambique

The book, hoe and rifle on the flag of Mozambique stand for education, farming and defence.

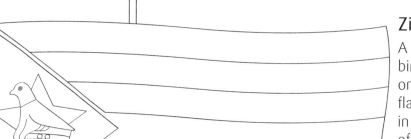

Zimbabwe

A stone-carved bird, like the one on this flag, was found in the ruins of the ancient city of Great Zimbabwe, from which the country took its name.

Egypt

The bird on the Egyptian flag is a golden eagle – the emblem of Saladin, a 12th-century Egyptian ruler. The writing says, 'Arab Republic of Egypt'.

Egypt

Eritrea

The emblem is an olive wreath, a symbol of peace. By law, Eritreans have to stand still if they pass the flag while it is being hoisted, and drivers must get out of their cars.

Eritrea

Morocco

Namibia

The sun on the Namibian flag symbolizes life and energy, while the blue stands for sky, green for land, red for the Namibian people, and white for peace and unity.

Namibia

Guinea-Bissau

39

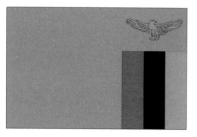

Zambia

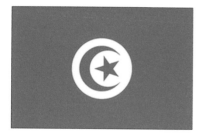

Tunisia

Comoros

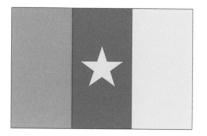

Cameroon

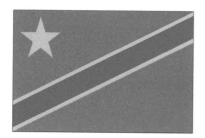

Congo
(Democratic Republic)

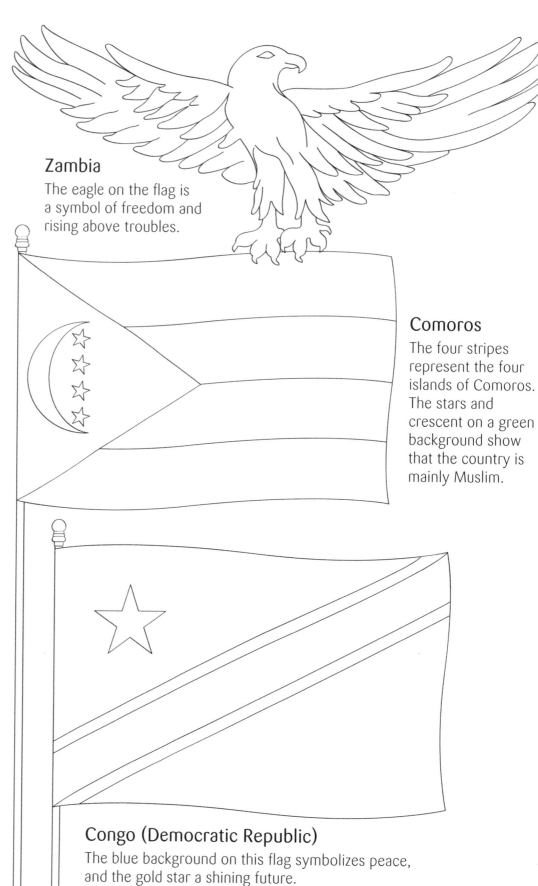

Zambia
The eagle on the flag is a symbol of freedom and rising above troubles.

Comoros
The four stripes represent the four islands of Comoros. The stars and crescent on a green background show that the country is mainly Muslim.

Congo (Democratic Republic)
The blue background on this flag symbolizes peace, and the gold star a shining future.

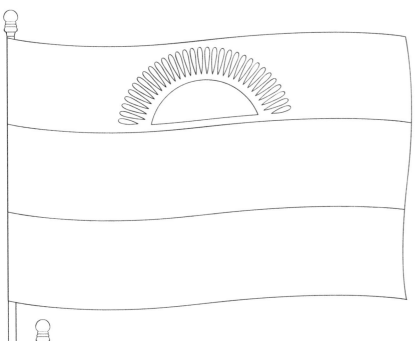

Malawi

The rising sun on the flag of Malawi stands for the dawn of hope and freedom for the whole of Africa.

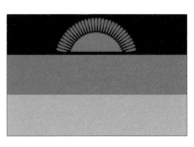

Malawi

Mali

Algeria

Central African Republic

This flag combines the Pan-African colours with the colours of the French flag, showing that the country was once a French colony.

Central African Republic

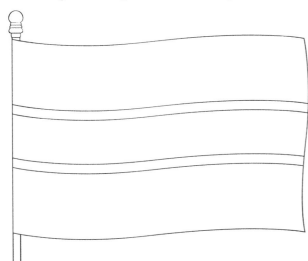

The Gambia

Red is for the sun and hot savannah, green for forests, and blue for the River Gambia.

The Gambia

Cape Verde

Togo

Equatorial Guinea

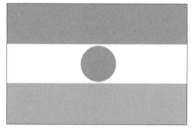

Niger

Guinea

South Sudan

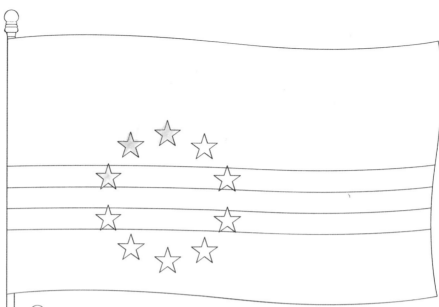

Cape Verde

The stars on this flag represent the ten islands that make up Cape Verde.

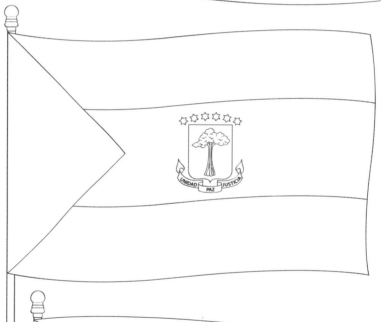

Equatorial Guinea

The coat of arms shows a silk cotton tree, under which a treaty is said to have been signed with Spain. The motto says, 'Unity, peace, justice' in Spanish.

South Sudan

This flag was only introduced in 2011, when South Sudan became independent from Sudan.

Benin

The colours of the flag of Benin are explained in the country's national anthem: green for hope, red for courage, and yellow for wealth.

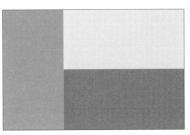

Benin

Tanzania

Tanzania

In 1964, the two countries of Tanganyika and Zanzibar united to form Tanzania. They also merged their flags to create this new one.

Uganda

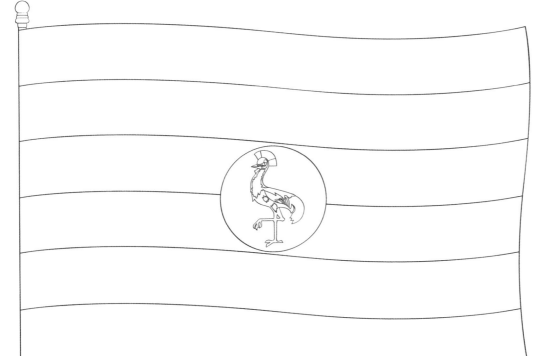

Uganda

The bird on the Ugandan flag is a crested crane, the country's national bird and emblem.

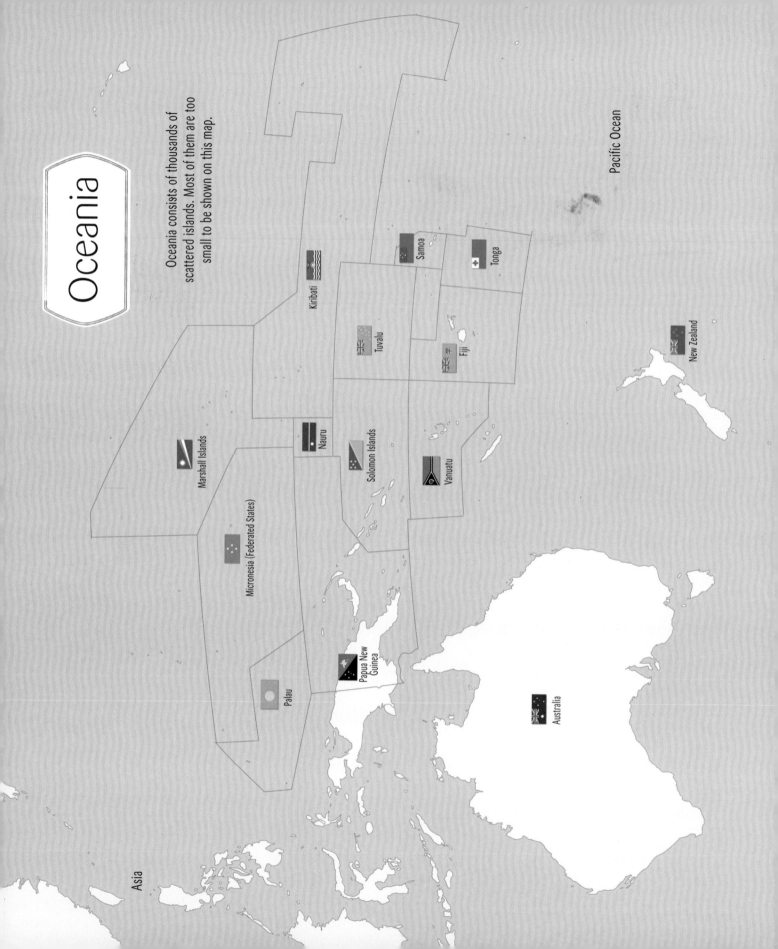

Oceania

Oceania consists of thousands of scattered islands. Most of them are too small to be shown on this map.

Pacific Ocean

Asia

Australia

New Zealand

Palau

Papua New Guinea

Micronesia (Federated States)

Marshall Islands

Nauru

Solomon Islands

Vanuatu

Kiribati

Tuvalu

Fiji

Samoa

Tonga

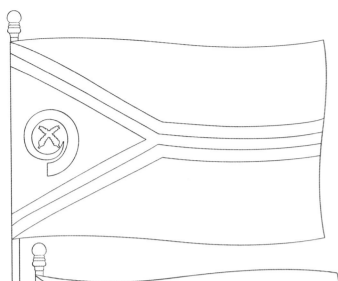

Vanuatu

The yellow Y-shape shows the pattern of the islands that make up Vanuatu. The swirl is a boar's tusk, a symbol of prosperity in the country. The fern fronds inside it stand for peace.

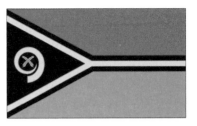

Vanuatu

Papua New Guinea

Papua New Guinea

A bird of paradise – Papua New Guinea's national bird – is shown on the flag, which was designed in a competition by a 15-year-old girl.

Samoa

Australia

Micronesia
(Federated States)

Australia

The five stars on the right show the Southern Cross, a pattern of stars seen in the night sky in the southern hemisphere. The biggest seven-pointed star stands for Australia's seven states and territories. The UK flag indicates that Australia used to be part of the British Empire.

Fiji

Tonga

New Zealand

Palau

Marshall Islands

Solomon Islands

Fiji

The coat of arms includes common Fijian crops: sugar cane, a coconut palm tree, bananas, and a cocoa pod, held in the lion's paws. The dove symbolizes peace.

Palau

The yellow circle on the Palauan flag is a full moon. According to tradition, this is the best time for community activities such as fishing, planting, harvesting and festivals.

Solomon Islands

On this flag, blue stands for the sea, green for the land, and yellow for the sun. The stars represent groups of islands.

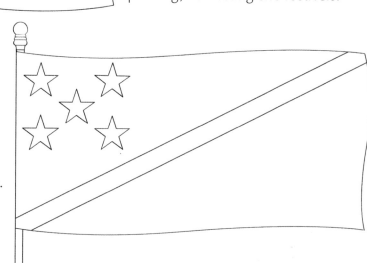

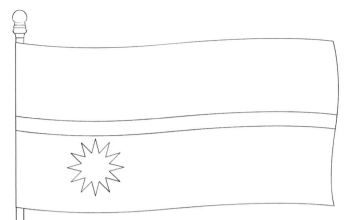

Nauru

Nauru lies only one degree south of the Equator, the imaginary line around the middle of the Earth. The yellow stripe represents the Equator, and the star the island's position.

Nauru

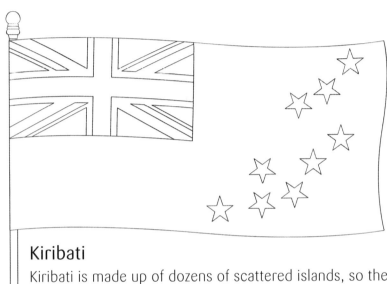

Tuvalu

The stars represent the nine islands of Tuvalu. The UK flag shows the country used to be in the British Empire.

Tuvalu

Kiribati

Kiribati is made up of dozens of scattered islands, so the sun is shown rising from the sea. The bird - a frigatebird - symbolizes power and freedom.

Kiribati

Usborne Quicklinks

For links to websites where you can find out more about flags, go to the Usborne Quicklinks website at www.usborne.com/quicklinks and type in the title of this book. Please follow the internet safety guidelines at the Usborne Quicklinks website. We recommend that children are supervised while on the internet.

Index

Usborne Publishing Ltd, 83-85 Saffron Hill, London, EC1N 8RT, United Kingdom.
First published in 2017. Copyright © 2017 Usborne Publishing Ltd. www.usborne.com
The name Usborne and the devices ♕🌐 are Trade Marks of Usborne Publishing Ltd.